T0387561

At the Fun Fair

Teaching Tips

Blue Level 4

This book focuses on the phonemes **/air/ure/**.

Before Reading

- Discuss the title. Ask readers what they think the book will be about. Have them briefly explain why.
- Ask readers to sort the words on page 3. Read the sounds and words together.

Read the Book

- Encourage readers to break down unfamiliar words into units of sound. Then, ask them to string the sounds together to create the words.
- Urge readers to point out when the focused phonics phonemes appear in the text.

After Reading

- Encourage children to reread the book independently or with a friend.
- Ask readers to name other words with /air/ or /ure/ phonemes. On a separate sheet of paper, have them write the words.

© 2024 Booklife Publishing
This edition is published by arrangement with Booklife Publishing.

North American adaptations © 2024 Jump!
5357 Penn Avenue South
Minneapolis, MN 55419
www.jumplibrary.com

Decodables by Jump! are published by Jump! Library.
All rights reserved. No part of this book may be reproduced in any form without written permission from the publisher.

Library of Congress Cataloging-in-Publication Data is available at www.loc.gov or upon request from the publisher.

ISBN: 979-8-88524-733-7 (hardcover)
ISBN: 979-8-88524-734-4 (paperback)
ISBN: 979-8-88524-735-1 (ebook)

Photo Credits

Images are courtesy of Shutterstock.com. With thanks to Getty Images, Thinkstock Photo and iStockphoto. Cover - Sinenkiy (foreground), photosmatic (background). 4-5 - Visun Khankasem, passion3. 6-7 - Gregory E. Clifford, clearviewstock. 8-9 - ZikG, Nic Vilceanu. 10-11 - Nigel Jarvis, Martin Charles Hatch. 12-13 - snowturtle, Hung Chung Chihg. 14-15 - Tomsickova Tatyana, MJTH. 16 - Shutterstock.

Can you sort the words on this page into two groups?

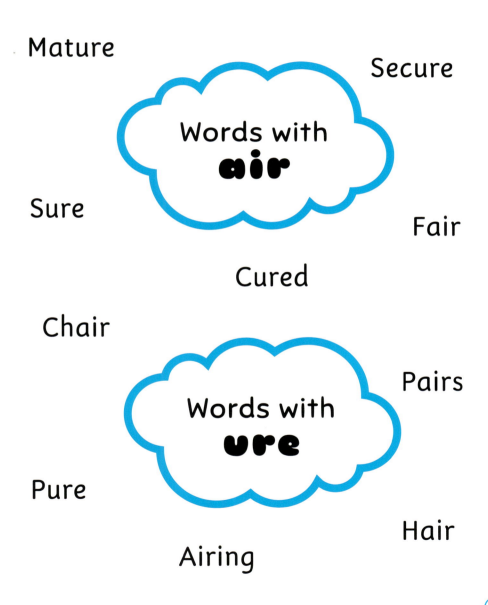

Mature

Secure

Sure

Fair

Cured

Chair

Pairs

Pure

Hair

Airing

We are at the fun fair! There are a lot of fun things to do.

Shall we start on the cups? This will be fun, for sure. We can spin!

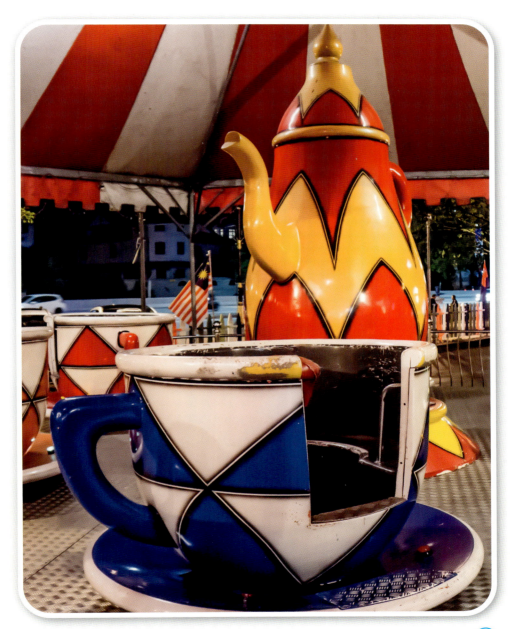

We might feel ill if we spin! Shall we go to the next thing?

It is a big fair!

Can you lure a duck with a stick?
Are you sure?

If you can lure a duck, you might win a prize!

Look in the air. It is high up. Up and down we go!

There is a bar. It will keep us secure in the chair.

It has a big loop high in the air.
I can feel the wind in my hair!

Shall we get on? We must be mature if we go that high in the air.

Wow! What a good sight! I can see cars, roads, and a farm.

Up the stairs and on to the cars next.
Go left and right and . . .

. . . BUMP!

What is the best part of the fair?

Sound out each word. Does it have an /air/ or /ure/ sound?

hair

picture

stairs

treasure